French Senegal: The History of the French Colony and Senegal's Transition to Independence

By Charles River Editors

A picture of Saint Louis, Senegal circa 1900

Introduction

Léopold Sédar Senghor

"The equilibrium you admire in me is an unstable one, difficult to maintain. My inner life was split early between the call of the Ancestors and the call of Europe, between the exigencies of black-African culture and those of modern life." - Léopold Sédar Senghor

Near the end of the 19th century, Otto von Bismarck, the German chancellor, brought the plenipotentiaries of all major powers of Europe together to deal with Africa's colonization in such a manner as to avoid provocation of war. This event, known as the Berlin Conference of 1884-1885, galvanized a phenomenon that came to be known as the Scramble for Africa. The conference established two fundamental rules for European seizure of Africa. The first of these was that no recognition of annexation would granted without evidence of a practical occupation, and the second, that a practical occupation would be deemed unlawful without a formal appeal for protection made on behalf of a territory by its leader, a plea that must be committed to paper in the form of a legal treaty.

This began a rush, spearheaded mainly by European commercial interests in the form of Chartered Companies, to penetrate the African interior and woo its leadership with guns, trinkets and alcohol, and having thus obtained their marks or seals upon spurious treaties, begin establishing boundaries of future European African colonies. The ease with which this was achieved was due to the fact that, at that point, traditional African leadership was disunited, and the people had just staggered back from centuries of concussion inflicted by the slave trade.

Thus, to usurp authority, to intimidate an already broken society, and to play one leader against the other was a diplomatic task so childishly simple, the matter was wrapped up, for the most part, in less than a decade. Even at that stage, however, the countries would keep jostling for position in Africa against each other, attempting to snap up more land and consolidate it. As such, the scramble kept going at a fevered pitch until the outbreak of World War I.

When they entered the negotiations in Berlin in 1884, the French were established in their flagship African territory of Senegal, situated at the westernmost point of continental Africa, which tended to give them an option over the vast reaches of the western continent so far unclaimed by any territory. The history of French engagement in Senegal can be traced back to 1677, with the French acquisition of a slave port on the island of Gorée, today a cantonment of the Senegalese capital of Dakar. From there, the French were apt to gaze across the vast expanse of unclaimed territory to their minor enclave of French Somaliland, founded between 1883 and 1887, and which would, in the post-independence era, become the state of Djibouti. The French imperial vision, therefore, became the establishment of French sovereignty over everything in between these two points, including, if possible, Egypt.

That vision ultimately clashed with British objectives, but somewhat ironically, conflicts against other enemies would ultimately determine how France's overseas empire was ultimately decolonized. In conjunction with those geopolitical events, certain influential individuals at home would be ready to fill in the European power vacuum while leading various independence movements, and one of these individuals was a poet and politician named Léopold Senghor.

French Senegal: The History of the French Colony and Senegal's Transition to Independence examines how France established the colony, and how that colony affected events in the 20th century before Senegal became a modern nation. Along with pictures depicting important people, places, and events, you will learn about French Senegal like never before.

French Senegal: The History of the French Colony and Senegal's Transition to Independence

About Charles River Editors
Introduction
The Birth of a Colony
Léopold Senghor and World War I
The Inter-War Period
The Impact of World War II
A Free Senegal
Françafrique
Online Resources
Further Reading
Free Books by Charles River Editors
Discounted Books by Charles River Editors

The Birth of a Colony

"My decision to destroy the authority of the blacks in Saint Dominque is not so much based on considerations of commerce and money, as on the need to block for ever the march of the blacks in the world." – Napoleon Bonaparte

Bearing in mind the proximity of France, Spain, and Portugal to the coast of north and northwest Africa, it stands to reason that the cultures of southern Europe and Africa would eventually collide. The first definite accounts of French maritime contact with the Atlantic coast of Africa came from French fishermen and merchants from the Normandy cities of Dieppe and Rouen. As early as the 12th century, French sailors ventured south into the waters off the coast of Mauritania, making occasional contact with Gambia and Senegal, and perhaps as far south as the Ivory and Gold Coasts. However, the Hundred Years War, which went on until the middle of the 15th century, tended to preoccupy France, leaving it largely to Portugal, as one of the leading maritime powers of the age, to push the business of exploring the coast of Africa incrementally, until, in 1488, the Portuguese mariner Bartolomeu Dias finally rounded the *Cabo das Tormentas*, or the "Cape of Storms," opening the first viable sea route to India.

In short order, the Portuguese founded the first permanent European trade centers along the coast of Senegal, establishing their base of operation in 1444 on the island of Gorée, a mile or so off the coast of what is today Dakar, the Senegalese capital. From there, slaves were traded, and they would continue to be traded for centuries.

In the ebb and flow of European wars and politics, powers rose and fell, and in 1588 the Dutch took Gorée and built a series of strong fortifications that allowed them to maintain the same deferential relationship with the local trading elites that the Portuguese previously did. The Dutch would not make any attempt to acquire sovereignty over the land, and aside from the horrible fates that befell millions of slaves, the relationship proved satisfactorily productive to both the Europeans and their trading partners.

The French appeared on the scene somewhat in 1659 by establishing their trade interests at the mouth of the Senegal River, at a place they named Saint Louis. Two decades later, thanks to events back in Europe, they superseded the Dutch at Gorée, acquiring an option over a territory that they would hold for the next 300 years aside from a brief interruption by the British. For over 200 years, the slave trade dominated, but by the first decade of the 19th century, the French had been compelled to cede to Britain's overarching goal of abolition.

A French depiction of their fort on Saint Louis

By then, the terms of the relationship between Europe and Africa were beginning to change. Abolition, and the British-led thrust to eradicate the international trade in slaves, tended to coincide with the industrialization of Europe, which brought an interest not only for raw materials, but also for new markets for European goods. This prompted a great deal of public interest in what lay in the African interior, and from their bases at the coast, the imperial powers of Europe began sponsoring expeditions aiming to explore and conquer the continent.

In 1825, the French fought their first minor war in Senegal, the Franco-Trarzan War. This was technically more of a French intervention in local wars between the Senegalese, but it marked the moment at which French sovereignty was established over a small, but growing hinterland surrounding Saint Louis. Private and official expeditions were periodically mounted up the Senegal River, which eventually took French explorers into the valley of the Upper Niger River, establishing an increasing range of territory as a French sphere of influence.

Meanwhile, the brief British interest in the region had no effect at all on expanding French influence along the coast of Senegal, nor did it affect the development of a cosmopolitan, French speaking population of mixed blood and native citizens who were loyal to France. In the view of most historians, this early contact and interaction between the French and natives in Senegal inspired the early French colonial policy of assimilation. It has also been noted that the French imperial theory at this time was influenced by the essential tenets of the French Revolution which tended to cast the whole process of imperialism under a more liberal and egalitarian light than found back in Britain or Portugal. As young Senegalese benefitting from this initial enthusiasm for assimilation were introduced into French schools, attitudes further liberalized, once again in stark contrast to the stiff and paternal attitude of the British towards their African imperial subjects.[1]

In the aftermath of the slave trade, Senegal languished economically and was developed only in the settled districts around Saint Louis, with imports tending to dominate the economy. In 1837, however, peanuts as a cash crop were introduced into the region, and this had the effect of stimulating the local economy and diversifying French interests into more general trade and in more thoughtful agricultural development.

Less than 20 years later, in 1854, a dynamic and forward-thinking governor named Louis Léon César Faidherbe was appointed to that post, and historians have since credited him with setting in motion the events that would lead to France's African empire. Faidherbe was a product of the lower middle classes in Lille. His military training was received first at the *École Polytechnique* and then at the *École d'Application* in Metz, after which he was rotated through numerous colonial postings before his transfer in 1852 to Senegal, as sub-director of engineers. It is probably worth noting that until the Berlin Conference of 1884, no real movement was made by any of the European powers to acquire and control large blocks of territory, although "natural hinterlands" and "spheres of influence" were very much part of the imperial verbiage of the era. The political will was nascent in the places where it did exist, and the challenges of geography and climate remained daunting. The British were established in the Cape and Natal, but they had yet to advance much further, and only the Portuguese, the earliest European colonizers, had bothered pretending to make a sovereign claim to any interior territory. The continent, for imperial purposes, remained wide open, and the nations of Europe awaited only the maturation of the imperial competition between them to begin the rapid advances that would characterize the 1880s and 1890s.

---

[1] The Portuguese also displayed a remarkable liberalism in regards to the sexual overlap of African and Portuguese in their colonies, but this was not seen, as it was by the French, as enriching black blood with white, but impoverishing white blood with black.

Faidherbe

It was Faidherbe who began to think in terms of advancing French interests and influence inland from Saint Louis, and of establishing Senegal as an administrative and logistical base for a much more ambitious advance inland. He sought to establish trade routes linking the coast with the Upper Niger River, which he correctly believed would divert the wealth of the trans-Sahara caravan routes into the French sphere. He was also acutely aware of the potential of British interest and competition in the region. After all, the British were established in various commercial enclaves along the coast, but most strongly at the mouth of the Niger River, which offered them a great deal of scope to dominate trade up the entire length of the Niger Basin. They also held territory in Sierra Leone, where slaves freed on the high seas were resettled. Closer to home, the British were entrenched at the mouth of Gambia River.

By then, the French settlement in Senegal had come to comprise what were known as the four *Communes* of Saint Louis, Gorée, Dakar, and Rufisque, each of which were essentially coastal enclaves of French urban aspects and administration in an otherwise unincorporated hinterland. The inhabitants of the *Communes*, regardless of color or creed, enjoyed full rights of French citizenship, and those of non-white origin were known as *évolué*, or the "civilized" in French imperial parlance. Outside the administrative boundaries of the *Communes*, however, no such rights existed.

At this point, the French policy of assimilation pictured, in ideal terms, the creation of a society of black Frenchmen in each of the French African colonies with equal rights to metropolitan French citizenship in territories designated as overseas provinces. The policy of assimilation, never more than an ideal, transmuted inevitably into a policy of association once the full scope of French African territory had been demarcated, and it became clear that creating 60 million Frenchmen in Africa was simply impractical. Assimilation, however, remained the preferred rule governing the overlap of the races in the four *Communes*, which meant that Senegal stood somewhat apart from France's other sub-Saharan imperial ventures, owning a status more in keeping with Algeria in its relationship with France.

Faidherbe did not achieve all of his goals, but he did establish Senegal itself as a solid, well administered and adequately policed and protected colony. Perhaps just as importantly, he helped develop it into a base for future French expeditions into the interior, even as his own efforts to reach the headwaters of the Niger River were blocked by unfriendly tribes and warlike kingdoms which would not be subdued for some time.

He also wasn't helped by the results of the Franco-Prussian War, which established a new power dynamic in Europe. Having been defeated by the Prussians and their allies, the French were now confronted with an enlarged and belligerent Germany, and France was justly fearful of any potential for confrontation with Britain. Thus, it was not until the 1880s that the French were sufficiently confident to begin thinking in terms of outward expansion from Senegal.

When that time came, two enormous, largely independent thrusts were mounted. The first involved French territories around the Mediterranean and the second, which involved the sub-Saharan territories, would be mounted from Senegal.

French sub-Saharan Africa was eventually expanded to include two vast federated blocks. The first was French West Africa, established in 1895 and comprising the territories of Senegal, Guinea, Côte d'Ivoire, French Sudan (later Mali), Mauritania, Niger, Upper Volta (later Burkina Faso) and Benin. The second was French Equatorial Africa, established in 1910 and comprising French Congo (Congo Brazzaville) and Gabon, Oubangui-Chari (Later Central African Republic), Chad and French Cameroon (after World War I). Each was governed from Paris through two Governors General, one based in Dakar and the other in Brazzaville, with Lieutenants Governor located in each territorial capital serving as deputies.

In 1877, Welsh American explorer Henry Morton Stanley emerged at the mouth of the Congo River, completing an expedition of 1,000 days to map the central lakes complex and explore the Congo River. Here was the definitive, Victorian template of African exploration. Stanley, known by the natives of the interior as *Bula Matari*, or the Breaker of Rocks, had left Zanzibar in 1874, traveling over land toward the continental divide, where his objective was to map the lakes of the Great Rift Valley, determine the source of the Nile, and explore the Lualaba River. Three years earlier, in 1871, Stanley made his name as an explorer through his successful search for Dr.

David Livingstone. Livingstone had not been heard from in Africa since departing England in 1866, also in search of the source of the Nile, and the general assumption was that he was dead.

Stanley

Livingstone

Stanley, however, while hardly shunning the publicity, had in mind much more than just the fame of a great explorer. His journey down the Congo River had alerted him to the fact that here lay a region ripe for commercial exploitation. The Congo River, for all its mythical isolation, was in fact easily navigable for most of its length, and it offered therefore the opportunity to any stout-hearted nation to exploit an almost unimaginable wealth of gold and ivory, the staples of African trade that had made so many fortunes already.

With a flair for self-aggrandizement, Stanley began immediately to lecture and publish, beginning in England but wending his way through all the great capitals of Europe. His mission was simply to urge any and all who would listen to seize the opportunity to claim the Congo and win for themselves not only the prodigious economic prize on offer, but also a great moral opportunity to stamp out the last embers of the East African Slave Trade, then flourishing in anonymity in the dark heart of Africa.

On the morning of Saturday, November 15, 1884, plenipotentiaries of all of the major powers of Europe gathered at the official residence of the German Reich Chancellor, Prince Otto von Bismarck. As each entered the yard, they were met at their carriage door by the Chancellor himself and then ushered into the library, where an informal reception took place. Then, as a body, they climbed the wide, ceremonial staircase to a second-floor reception room, where each took his allocated seat at a semi-circular table arranged before a large and detailed map of Africa pinned to the wall. Bismarck addressed the assembled delegates, outlining briefly the objectives of the meeting, after which, casting his eyes from left to right, he declared the Berlin Conference formally in session.

Bismarck

A depiction of Bismarck at the Berlin Conference

The Berlin Conference of 1884-85, a dry and rather formal affair, was nonetheless one of the most important and far-reaching gatherings of international power to take place at any time during the 19th century, and one that would deeply impact the course of European and African history up to the present day. In its simplest terms, the Berlin Conference sought to regulate the subdivision of Africa between the principal European powers in a manner that would not cause a major war between them. Only a somewhat desultory European interest had been shown in Africa to date, amounting to little more than a patchwork of competing spheres of influence. These were mostly private concerns — chartered companies displaying a national flag — but here and there, territories were being annexed and occupied, and in general, a rather unhealthy mood of competition was incubating over the question of Africa.

Perhaps the best example of this was the Witwatersrand, the gold-bearing region of the Transvaal Republic, nominally a British sphere of influence and certainly the most important theatre of British capital adventure of the age. South Africa at that point was divided into four separate territories - two British colonies (Natal and Cape) and two independent Boer republics (Transvaal and Orange Free State) - and between these there existed enormous suspicion and antipathy. The superior weight of British capital and imperial reach allowed the British to dominate the Transvaal gold fields, but they did so very much to the chagrin of the Boer. The Boer were not by any means impoverished because of this, but as they prospered, they were ever vigilant toward any British threat against their sovereignty.

It was onto this rather tense economic and political stage that the Germans entered in 1884, annexing the territory of Damaraland, nominally the whole of modern-day Namibia, as a German colony. This immediately pitched the British into a fit of apprehension. What were German intentions? Was it the gold, the diamonds, the strategic ports, or all of the above? The British were acutely aware that the hatred felt toward them by the Boer could easily drive them into the arms of an opposing European power, and bearing in mind the ideological compatibility of Germany and Boer at that time, the Germans were in a position, should they choose, to wreak havoc on British interests in South Africa.

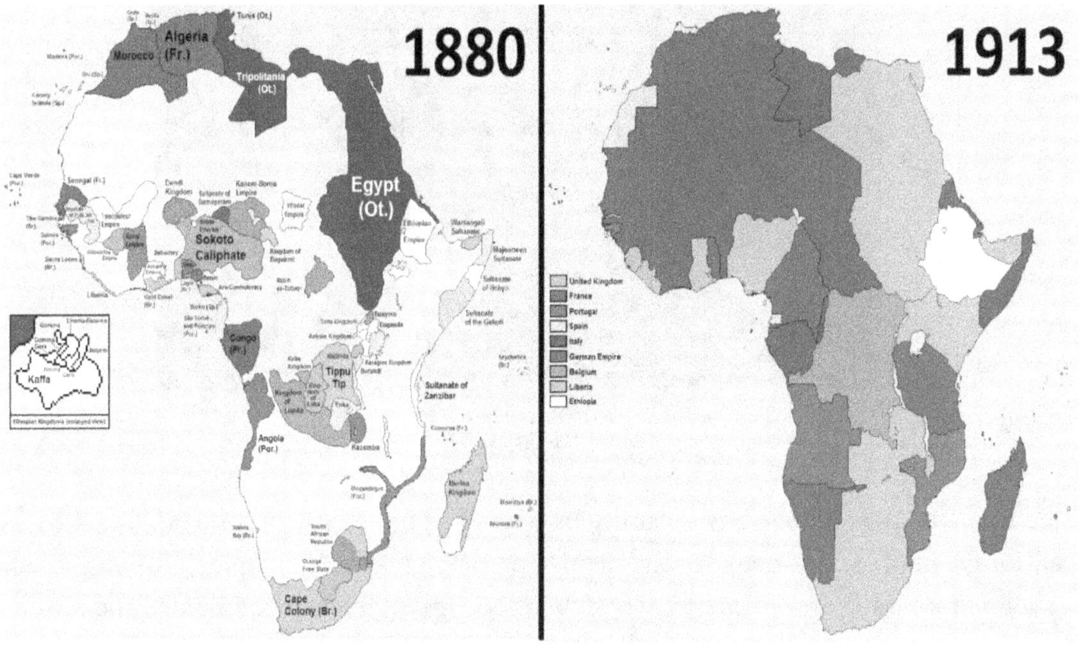

A map of African colonies in 1880 and 1913

Just a few years before the conference, in 1877, a young and wealthy British adventurer and ex-officer of the Royal Engineers was obliged to make himself scarce in England due to sexual and social impropriety. To allow the dust to settle, George Taubman Goldie embarked on a journey to Africa, and at some point he found himself at the mouth of the Niger River, a hive of international trade activity since the earliest days of the West African gold and slave trade. Goldie was 31, and his ostensible objective on the Niger River was to inspect a minor trading concern owned by his family that dealt primarily in palm oil products and was competing in this trade with a multitude of small and medium-sized concerns, primarily of French and British origin. A cursory survey of the region convinced Goldie that this was a land of opportunity, assuming, of course, that he could achieve a monopoly.

Goldie

Goldie took over this branch of the family business and quickly went to work neutralizing his competition. A man of enormous daring, he also possessed both financial genius and a ruthless streak, and before long he was mopping up underperforming trading companies and absorbing their supply networks. Soon he began to accumulate and bear down on the bigger players. In 1897 he formed the United Africa Company with a nominal capital of £250,000, a sizable sum at the time, and he formalized a general merger that could practically guarantee a British trade monopoly on the Niger River.

Goldie went about his plans, but he wasn't the only one there, and the region had a long history of international trade and would not turn British as easily as Goldie hoped. By 1890, the British position on the natural hinterland of the Niger comprised a colony of convenience known as the Lagos Colony, along with a rather amorphous entity known as the Niger Coast Protectorate, which had no administrative structures and no northern perimeter. Trade was conducted with established indigenous mercantile networks that were both organized and wealthy. In the aftermath of abolition, trade transitioned easily from slaves to oil palm products, and since trade was conducted along the river, that tended to be the only point of contact. The whites were typically referred to by local traders as "fish" because they were always reluctant to leave the water.

Goldie then girded himself to deal with his French competitors. Business interests didn't necessarily toe a patriotic or nationalist line, so Goldie figured negotiating a French exit from the region was simply a matter of discussion, perhaps aided by minor trade wars only when necessary. In 1882, Goldie floated the National African Company with a nominal capital of £1,000,000, and from there he began to aggressively push his trade hinterland outward, for the first time using armed force and securing a kind of administrative control over large areas simply to keep the peace. Thus, when Britain participated in the Berlin Conference, Goldie had essentially set the stage for a viable British claim to the region, and the British claims to the Lagos Colony and the Niger Coast Protectorate were duly recognized.

Now that they were pushed off the Niger, the French established themselves next door in the old slave trading entrepôt Dahomey, modern-day Benin. In the aftermath of the Berlin Conference, hardened attitudes regarding who was where and who had a right to what began to influence British and French officials in their respective West African enclaves. The northern limits of these respective spheres of influence remained undefined and technically open to the first comer, so both sides began a rapid and often acrimonious push to extend their respective influences northwards. The time had come to prove effective occupation and administration, and the first to do so would, according to the rules of the game, have first claim over any new territory.

The issue of how the British would administer the land Goldie was operating in was determined in 1886 when Goldie was awarded with a royal charter. His company, thereafter known as the Royal Niger Company, became the first of three significant British private companies to influence the course of British imperialism in Africa. The second was Rhodes' British South Africa Company, which would govern the colonies that became Northern Rhodesia and Southern Rhodesia, and the third was the Imperial British East Africa Company.

Goldie was limited by economic necessity to overseeing a very superficial administration, which demonstrated the fundamental difference between the French and British styles of imperialism. In the late 1880s and early 1890s, Britain's imperial drive was inhibited by a succession of Liberal and fiscally cautious Conservative governments reluctant to commit public resources to major expansion in Africa. As a result, private commercial and missionary activities defined early British spheres of influence and drove them forward. Sierra Leone, for example, existed simply as an enclave from which to launch Royal Navy anti-slavery operations in the North Atlantic and resettle slaves liberated on the high seas. The Gold Coast (modern Ghana) existed at that time as a British trading concession and did not acquire the status of a British protectorate until 1902.

France, on the other hand, tended to take a grand, continental-scale view of Africa, and, backed by powerful government and private interests, the French sought to exploit the Scramble for

Africa to acquire a portion of the landmass commensurate with their material assets. They achieved this in West Africa, and in that part of the continent they controlled more ground than the British.

The major exception was Nigeria, the largest British colony in West Africa, and the point from where the British took a stand. The French, established in the territory of Dahomey (modern-day Benin), began challenging British control of the navigable portions of the Niger River by probing outwards into a region known broadly as Borgu, whose capital was the unknown and unvisited city of Nikki.[2] This resulted in a great deal of diplomatic jostling and unpleasantness back in London and Paris, but it also extended into the field in Africa, where the Royal Niger Company's soldiers occasionally confronted French imperial troops. It's important to remember that on both sides, the soldiers were indigenous natives - the French made use of Senegalese *Tirailleurs*, and the Royal Niger Company's Hausa men at arms were recruited from the northern emirates above the Niger-Benue confluence.

In 1889, the two sides met, as they did on occasion, to resolve an issue that still had the potential to ignite a war. The result was the Anglo-French Agreement of 1889 which, among other territorial issues, defined the boundary between French Dahomey and the Lagos Colony. A point was demarcated more or less where the coastal modern boundary between Benin and Nigeria stands today, and from that point, an imaginary line was drawn as far as the ninth parallel north. This is a distance of about 200 miles, and it served as an agreed upon land border.

Léopold Senghor and World War I

"The civilization of the twentieth century cannot be universal except by being a dynamic synthesis of all the cultural values of all civilizations. It will be monstrous unless it is seasoned with the salt of negritude, for it will be without the savor of humanity." - Léopold Sédar Senghor

By the turn of the 20th century, all but a handful of African states and kingdoms had fallen under European domination, with a system of ports ringing the continent while a network of roads, telegraph and railway lines cut ever deeper into the interior. The continent had been divided up into allied administrative units, each with a local government and judiciary, and some, like the main settled colonies, had quite sophisticated, self-governing political establishments.

It was in those territories, including French Senegal, but also places like Kenya, Rhodesia, and South Africa, that the greatest opportunities for black advancement existed. Senegal offered a wide scope of opportunity for education, and for employment thereafter. Both the church and the state provided education facilities (often non-segregated) to young blacks from established family backgrounds, and the bureaucracy, the army, the police, and private industry all offered

---

[2] Nikki is today a small city in north-eastern Benin.

avenues of employment and advancement. This does not imply that all French overseas territories were governed in this manner, because that was certainly not the case, but the *Communes* of Senegal were unique, and within them existed arguably the most liberal, enlightened colonial regime of the era.

On October 9, 1906, a child was born in the Senegalese coastal town of Joal, on the southern coast of the colony, lying about 40 miles south of Dakar, the main *commune* and territorial capital. The child's name was Léopold Sédar Senghor, and by virtue of his birth outside of the *Communes*, he began his life as a French subject, not a French citizen. His background was reasonably commonplace insofar as he was born into the family of a prosperous, middle-class trader. He was the son of a junior wife who happened to be a Fulani of the Muslim faith, but the family as a whole identified as Christian.

His formal education, as it did for a majority of well-to do-Senegalese youth, began at a mission school run by the local chapter of the Catholic Marist "White Fathers." He was immersed in a literary style of education, with an emphasis on understanding the gospels, and he was also exposed to Catholicism in a society generally accommodating of religion, with a reasonably evenly balanced representation of Christianity and Islam.

The Catholic fathers were always on the lookout for exceptional native youth to induct into the church, and as a pious and studious child, Senghor was identified almost immediately as a likely prospect. At that time, entering the Catholic Church as a novice was something to aspire to, for it offered a career far above the usual fare of the military or civil service. Thus, at the age of 17, Léopold Senghor was enrolled in the recently opened Libermann Seminary in Dakar, alongside 15 other boys, most of whom were white.

This was an auspicious time for a young, black Senegalese to be starting his advanced education in a French overseas territory. In the wake of the ghastly Great War, a more liberal and idealistic French generation began to come of age. The empire was now progressively seen less as a vehicle for inter-European political and commercial competition and more as the means to create a more meaningful and utopian world. A central theme of this concept was an obligation to nurture the abilities and aspiration of the indigenous youth of the empire, which also happened to correspond with the advent of the indigenous peoples' political consciousness throughout imperial Africa. The war itself did not directly impact Senegal, or any of the French West African territories, other than the deployment of large numbers of Senegalese *Tirailleurs* to various active fronts. Throughout the French imperial period in Africa, the Senegalese *Tirailleurs* were almost invariably the troops of choice, and they saw action in World War I, World War II, and several colonial conflicts.[3] The *Tirailleurs* were a professional and highly

---

[3] During World War I, five Senegalese battalions saw action on the Western Front, while others were deployed in garrison duty across the French Maghreb. French Senegalese *Tirailleurs* were included in the orders of battle in Ypres and Dixmude during the *Battle of Flanders* of late 1914, at the capture of Fort de Douaumont in October 1916, during the battle of Chemin des Dames in April 1917 and at the Battle of Reims in 1918. Later, in 1915, seven battalions were deployed to the Dardanelles, and later still, some 40,000 colonial troops were used in the occupation of Rhineland.

regarded unit of the combined French armed forces. Those who served in World War I returned to the colony changed by the experience, and they were given much food for thought when they discovered that white men could just as easily be killed in battle as black men.

One enlightened product of the wartime era was Governor General Joost van Vollenhoven, who was Dutch-born and had French citizenship. He arrived in Dakar in the spring of 1917, and though he was just 40, van Vollenhoven had already accrued considerable military and diplomatic experience.

Van Vollenhoven

Van Vollenhoven only served in the post for a year before being ordered to the Western Front in the summer of 1918 to take part in the Battle of Reims (where he was killed in action), but he was responsible for a handful of significant reforms. For example, van Vollenhoven may have been most responsible for altering the essential philosophical underpinning of French imperialism from "assimilation" to "association," claiming that assimilation was not only impractical, but also undesirable. There was nothing to be gained, he said, by the expectation that a native of Africa identify absolutely and completely with France in order to be absorbed into a "Greater France." Instead, he believed it would be far better if the best parts of both cultures were encouraged to emerge, thereby creating a society where the French and natives "associated" to the advantage of both. This would create a hybrid culture, without the requirement of choosing between one or the other.

Perhaps not surprisingly, the idea was not popularized simply for reasons of fairness to the cultural value of French Africans. In France, the new philosophy of Social Darwinism tended to set the black man of Africa on a lower evolutionary scale than whites, and a pervasive belief that the two races were fundamentally incompatible certainly did drive some schools of imperial thought. It also dawned on plenty of Frenchmen that trying to include every black African into the French social charter was not only impractical, but potentially deadly to France's own independence and culture.

As a result, the policy of assimilation the French did utilize became highly selective, and only a handful of gifted young men, like Léopold Sédar Senghor, would be trusted with free and inhibited access to the great institutions of France. It was assumed such students would ultimately come away with a cultural and social investment in France, and that they could thus subsequently be relied upon to lead the masses of their colonies in a way that retained loyalty to France. As von Vollenhoven himself put it, the elite native class "must evolve more and more in our environment."

For reasons never explicitly explained (but probably because of willfulness and a streak of independent thought), young Senghor was eventually guided out of religious education and into a newly founded secular school in Dakar, aptly named van Vollenhoven Lycée. He excelled there, graduating after six years and having won almost every academic award and endowment on offer. He easily exceeded the academic standards necessary for the grant of an official scholarship to study in France.

The man who lobbied on Senghor's behalf to gain a scholarship and then helped Senghor overcome the resistance of his deeply conservative father was the local director of education, Aristide Prat. Prat was another enlightened colonial administrator, at least in the context of his era, and he was keenly interested in the promotion of indigenous talent in the colonies. With Prat's help, Léopold Sédar Senghor embarked on a new chapter in 1928. He was only 21, but as it turned out, he would soon alter the course of France and Africa permanently.

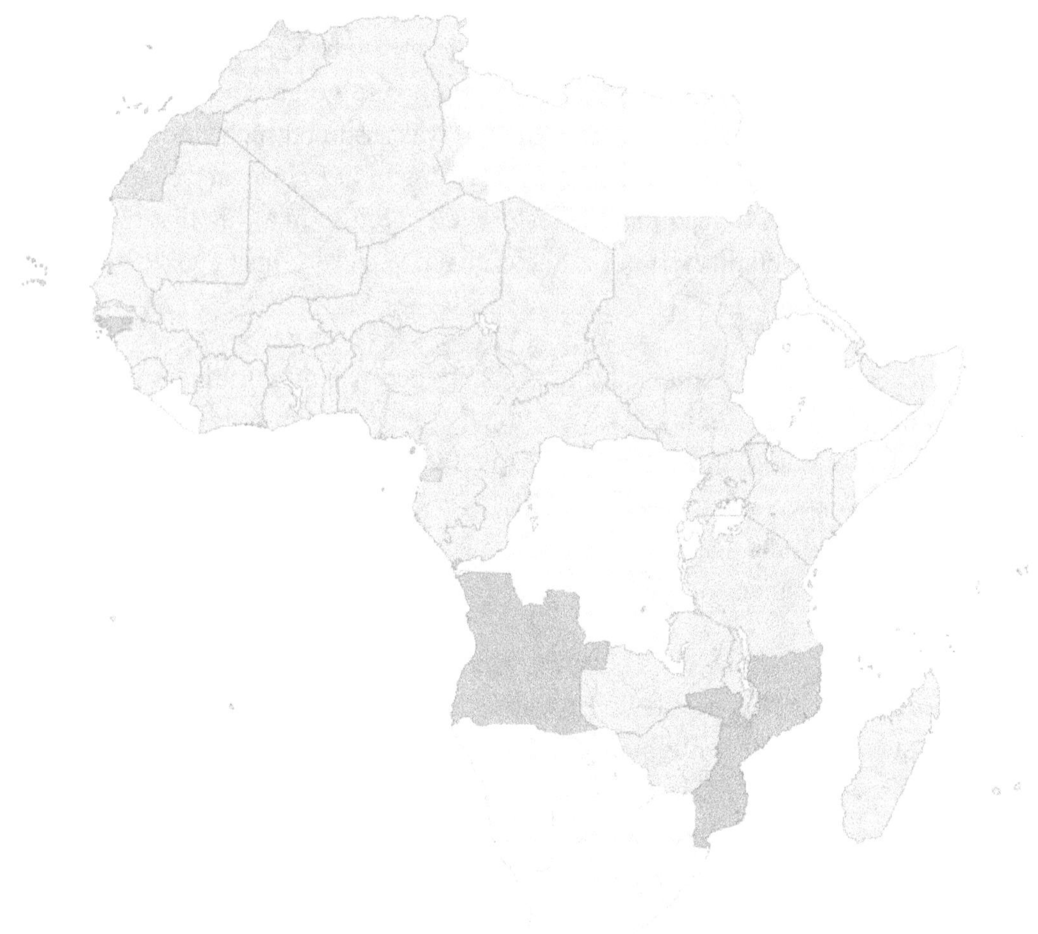

A map of the different African colonies in 1930, with France's in blue

"I believe if the white and colored people could get together and be let alone, they would understand each other and consequently love each other." – Josephine Baker

Léopold Senghor's arrival in Paris in 1928 could hardly have been better timed. This was the Paris of the Jazz Age, the *Paris Noir* of Josephine Baker, of Hemingway's *A Moveable Feast*, of Picasso and Jean-Paul Sartre. While it was a society weighed down by the continent's growing militancy and the polarization of political ideology, it was also a society energized by a renewed philosophical and artistic vigor, by race integration, social and sexual libertarianism, and wide-ranging challenges to many of the established social doctrines of the past. The perceived color blindness of Parisian society at this time attracted thousands of African and African-American intellectuals, as well as blacks from French colonies as diverse as Madagascar, Martinique, Guyana, French Guiana, and the wide scope of the French Caribbean. At the same time, the

Harlem Renaissance, which marked an explosion of black intellectual, social, and artistic expression in the Harlem district of Manhattan, also influenced Paris, where many of the leading figures of the movement settled permanently or visited to enlarge and enrich the wider movement.

The comparative liberalism of France at this time was first noticed by black American servicemen deployed to Europe during World War I. James Reese Europe, an African-American military bandsman and ragtime composer, was captivated by the atmosphere of acceptance that he and his bandmates encountered in Paris, which was so radically different from back home in the United States. Later, numbers of black American artists, writers, composers and musicians, like James Baldwin, Augusta Savage, Josephine Baker, and others, would find similar acceptance and acclaim in France.

Another side to this environment of free racial integration flourished in Paris. Though it was somewhat less obvious to the French, this integration led to conversations and relationships forged by blacks from different parts of the empire as they gathered in Paris to study, immerse themselves in international culture, and share ideas like pan-Africanism, black cultural autonomy, and African liberation. Many, like Senghor, were arriving in Paris not from America, but from the French colonies, taking similar advantage of scholarships, entering schools and universities, utilizing a flowering of opportunity and the many avenues of intellectual artistic expression on offer. The comparative sophistication of African-American expatriates, perhaps more militant politically than those like Senghor, but certainly accomplished and of independent spirit, inspired a parallel black African and Caribbean intellectual and political movement, one that certainly had no parallel anywhere else in the current European imperial environment.

This environment had been fairly well established by the time Senghor arrived in the winter of 1928. Though he was in awe and isolated, he was guided through the early stages by the established doyen of the black Senegalese community, 56-year-old Blaise Diagne. Diagne was a remarkable figure who had, since 1914, served in the French Chamber of Deputies as the elected representative of the four *Communes* of Senegal. One need only reflect on the imperial philosophies of the other major European players to appreciate how extraordinary it was that a native-born black African enjoyed a permanent and respected seat in the French imperial legislature. Such a thing would have been unimaginable in Britain at the time, and even less so in imperial Portugal or Germany. An Indian Member of Parliament, Dadabhai Naoroji, served briefly in the British House of Commons in the late 1890s, but he represented a metropolitan British constituency, not a native Indian constituency, and there was certainly no precedent for a black member to represent a colonial protectorate in a central legislature.

Diagne

Diagne was a product of the domestic political establishment in Senegal, rising through the ranks of the civil service and later serving as the first black mayor of Dakar. He was a staunch advocate of assimilation, being afforded and enjoying the respect, opportunities, and financial rewards that might be expected of any Frenchman in his position. It certainly would be argued by some in subsequent decades that he had become somewhat too integrated and enamored with life in Paris, and too much at peace with the benefits of his French identity. Diagne was exactly the type of individual van Vollenhoven envisioned when coming up with his more liberal cultural assimilation ideals, but W.E.B. Du Bois, an occasional visitor to Paris, described Diagne as a Frenchman who was accidentally black. Diagne was described by some of the French themselves as our "blackest deputy," which was meant to be affectionate. Diagne could be upheld as living proof of the success of the French assimilation policy, even though it was very selectively applied. Diagne himself has been quoted as asserting, "We French natives wish to remain French, since France has given us every liberty and since she has unreservedly accepted us on the same basis as her European children. None of us want to see French Africa given over exclusively to Africans."

Meanwhile, Senghor began attending lectures at the Sorbonne, and in due time he entered Lycée Louis-le-Grand, widely regarded as the most rigorous and celebrated secondary school in France. He read literature at the Sorbonne in preparation for a career as a teacher, but as the decade waned and the Great Depression stripped away some of the gaiety of the Roaring Twenties, he began to develop an increasingly active political identity. By the 1930s, as the concept of African liberation began to truly take root, young students like Senghor began increasingly to concern themselves with the meaning of being black in the modern world.

Around this time, Senghor made a number of key social connections, perhaps the most important of which was Aimé Césaire, a gifted black student from the French Caribbean island of Martinique. Another was Léon Damas, a student hailing from French Guiana. For both of these men, Senghor was the first African black man they met who was their intellectual equal, and through them Senghor was introduced into the diverse black communities of Paris, in particular the West Indian community. Particularly influential in that fraternity were the Nardal Sisters, Jane, Paulette and Andreé, each wealthy, well connected, artistic, and black.

Césaire

Paulette Nardal

It was through these new social connections, in particular the Nardal sisters, that Senghor heard about both the Harlem Renaissance and the New Negro Movement, and he began to actively meet and mingle with influential Africans, other black colonials, and African-Americans. At this time, the first journal of black expression in Paris, the short lived *La Revue du Monde Noir,* was published to a wide and discerning audience. This publication, through the underlying theme that all blacks, no matter what their cultural origins, experienced a common interest, hoped to generate a worldwide black consciousness. Although it ultimately did not achieve its goals, it certainly built upon a growing body of independent black expression.

Senghor also read and was influenced by Alain Locke's 1925 *New Negro Anthology,* which he was able to get a French translation of in 1932. Locke, a Harvard graduate and the first ever black Oxford Rhodes Scholar, was recognized as the unofficial "Dean of the Harlem Renaissance," giving the movement a philosophical and academic profile.

Senghor held his position in this movement mostly because he represented black Africa, as opposed to African-American and Afro-Caribbean "blackness," which, while better established, was not considered authentically African by contemporaries. He also offered up an intellectual gravitas that, although never quite of the caliber of Alain Locke, was nonetheless remarkable. He also happened to be a great deal less militant than his American peers since he could hardly risk offending the authorities when it was through their agency that he was able to live and study in Paris at all. It is perhaps also true that he did necessarily not feel that kind of political militancy, for never had he experienced the difficulties of racism that black Americans had, for in both

Senegal and Paris, Senghor had been unhindered by any overt or destructive racism.

Locke

One must be careful to remember the context of Senghor's moderate experience and gilded journey, for it represented conditions only in the *Communes* of Senegal, not the commonplace experience of the *originaires* of the rest of French Africa. A man who would emerge as Senghor's revolutionary colleague and frequent political rival, Félix Houphouët-Boigny, was experiencing in Côte d'Ivoire a more traditional black African experience. In all of their overseas territories, the French applied what can perhaps best be described as a variable system of indirect rule. Under the general French system, expatriate administrative personnel ran their various districts by seconding local leadership. The British also employed a similar device, but as history has tended to judge, they did so with a far greater sensitivity to local tradition and leadership than the French. The British emphasized an "advisory" role in local and domestic politics and law, most effectively in such places as Nigeria, while the French were much more prone to applying a "supervisory" role which was less popular (and some would say less effective). The French did not always respect established lines of succession, and they would reward or punish individual aspirants by imposing or denying their presences upon the various seats of traditional authority.

Houphouët-Boigny happened to be so favored, and his education was taken over by the colonial authorities to prepare him for district leadership, but at no time was he considered for a scholarship to study overseas. He qualified as a doctor at the French West Africa School of Medicine in Côte d'Ivoire, but only as a second-class doctor – he would never have been on course to treat a white patient, and he would never enjoy the right or license to practice in France.

Houphouët-Boigny

The Impact of World War II

"France is not alone! She is not alone! She has a great empire behind her!" – General Charles de Gaulle

The start of World War II was a watershed moment for European imperialism. World War I had destroyed four of the world's most influential empires, leaving the British, French and Portuguese empires standing, but critically weakened. World War II, in turn, broke the back of these three surviving empires and would lead to imminent liberation for imperial subjects across the world.

At the same time, the French recruited and deployed large numbers of African servicemen for frontline duty in many theatres. This tended to expose a progressive generation of young men to ideas of liberation and freedom from tyranny, in particular those who served under French colors. Among British subjects, a majority served in Southeast Asia and were regularly furloughed and retrained in India, where the "Quit India" independence movement was being driven forward with unstoppable momentum. All of this tended to nurture and inspire a sense of pending independence among young Africans, who lacked only the caliber of leadership of men such as Gandhi and Nehru to lead the masses into action.

It also so happened, however, that this corps of homegrown African leaders was coming into its own. The 1940s witnessed the coming of age of the first highly educated generation of black African students who were beginning to drift back from foreign universities with the first crop of indigenous African master's degrees and PhDs. These individuals were generally disinclined towards assimilation, association or any such identification with a foreign occupying power. They were fully conversant in modern political theory, educated, sophisticated, unafraid to challenge the system, and confident in their ability to govern independent nations.

At the outbreak of war, Senghor was teaching at a French secondary school in Tours in the southwest of France, and as a French citizen it was taken for granted that he would volunteer for service and fight for his country. Thus, in 1939, he enlisted as a private in the 59th Colonial Infantry Division, but he was promptly captured almost as soon as the German invasion was launched, spending a total of two years in various prison camps within France. Much of his time as a POW was spent writing poetry, the bulk of which would comprise his first published volume, *Chants d'ombre* (*Shadow Songs*), published in 1945.

He was released in 1942 on medical grounds, after which he resumed teaching, and although some have asserted he was part of the French Resistance, this doesn't appear to be true. In reality, Senghor apparently passed the remainder of the war reasonably quietly. Ironically, the momentous events that would shape his future and that of French Africa were being played out much closer to Senegal than Tours.

During World War II, the Free French movement retained the pride and dignity of France at a time when France itself lay under occupation, and its government was in open collaboration with the Nazis. Free France was a powerful idea — the concept of a state retaining its sovereignty in the face of invasion. The French knew, however, and General Charles de Gaulle himself knew too, that it was Africa that had made this possible.

De Gaulle

The French Empire in Africa, or *France Outre-Mer*, comprised two vast territorial blocs, French Equatorial Africa and French West Africa. During the early phases of the war, French West Africa allied itself with the Vichy regime, while French Equatorial Africa sided with the Free French. Free French headquarters were established in Brazzaville, the capital of French Congo, and from there General de Gaulle sustained a government in exile. Loyalties would begin to shift, however, as the fortunes of war tilted, and by the end of 1942, as German and Italian troops evacuated from Tunisia, all of French Africa had declared for the Free French.

During the war, the Vichy government and Free France competed for favor in African eyes. The decisions were not African decisions to make, of course, because French Africa was not under African control, but the symbolism of Africa saving the dignity of France was powerful. Moreover, the 200,000 or so African soldiers who served on the Free French and Allied sides during the war cemented a strong bond of affection. General de Gaulle's eventual victory in securing French Africa to his cause also tended to offer a final vindication of the value of overseas power in securing France's position in Europe.

The most important and most interesting effect of all of this was psychological. France had suffered defeat and occupation by Germany, and notwithstanding the fact that large numbers of French remained either supine or actively in collaboration with the Nazis, due recognition was given to General de Gaulle and the Free French movement for maintaining French national integrity in the face of the Nazi occupation. Moreover, it was acknowledged that French Africa in general, and Equatorial Africa in particular, had offered a platform upon which the Free French movement had been able to exist. France had remained whole thanks to Africa, and moreover, if France was to remain a major global power after the war, *France Outre-Mer* was of even greater importance.

Unfortunately for the French, the rest of the world was moving towards decolonization, and the French were apt (or resigned) to acknowledge this. The first of the major French dominos to fall was French Indochina, which was lost largely consequent to the signature French military defeat at Dien Bien Phu in 1954.[4] This was a precursor to the Vietnam War, and although it lingers in popular French memory as a humiliating defeat, it would prove less politically significant to the fate of the French Empire than the Algerian War that followed four years later.

The Algerian Crisis erupted in 1958, and it was this signature event that brought the issue of decolonization in Africa to the very forefront of the French political debate. The French Algerian Crisis was a complex and multi-faceted emergency that played out on the French doorstep and affected a territory that the French felt a strong fraternal bond with. The demands for independence emanating from Algeria struck at the very core of the French identity as an imperial power, and French resistance to it bordered at times on the fanatical. It also tended to highlight the inherent instability of the Fourth Republic, and into a political impasse in 1958, largely informed by Algeria, de Gaulle returned to national politics. He dissolved the constitution of the Fourth Republic and founded the Fifth Republic, established on more decisive principals and committed to a more comprehensive policy of decolonization.

One of de Gaulle's first actions upon taking the office of Prime Minister (and shortly afterward as President of the Republic) was to implement a new constitution that would allow for autonomous "colonies" to claim a place as members of a French Union. Years of emotional debate preceded this first deliberate step toward the devolution of the Empire. Many eminent thinkers and policymakers contributed to it, but perhaps none quite so eloquently as Senghor himself. The essence of his view was that once the more destructive features of both European

---

[4] The *First Indochina War* lasted for over 7-years, from 1946 to 1954.

imperialism and black nationalism had been curbed, each could join in a natural and equal polarity. Senghor remarked, "The Europe that must be created does not stop in Marseilles or Sicily. It is in reality two continents which are complimentary, that is Europe and Africa, in reality it is a political, economic and cultural eurafrican community which must be formed."

Many similar contributions were made to the debate — some emotive, others fanciful, and yet others eminently sensible — but it was one man, de Gaulle, who ultimately managed the transition and defined its practical parameters. His sense of the future was informed by the recent past, and by the role that Africa had played in supporting the Free French. The general post-war sense that France was to Africa what Samson was to his hair in the Bible was to de Gaulle a matter of fact, not legend. However, external factors – the expectations of the Atlantic Charter, the wars in Algeria and Indochina, and a general shift in the global power equation – tended to impose an agenda on de Galle that, like Churchill, was not always to his taste. At the same time, decolonization in the manner being undertaken by the British – an ignominious retreat based around a profound collapse of belief – was not the pattern that either de Gaulle or the French wished to follow.

In the post-war period, the French considered simply the redrafting of the original imperial design, not a renunciation of it. The French Union, in its infant form, was established by Title Eight of the Constitution of the Fourth Republic. The preamble to this ran as follows: "France together with the overseas peoples shall form a union founded upon equality of rights and duties, without distinction of race or religion." This moderate language was obscured by the more detailed articles that followed, which tended to define differing standards of membership in the union, all of which served generally to ensure the durability of France's past colonial legacy. Nonetheless, it was a creative and pragmatic solution to the problem, and with typical élan, de Gaulle moved ahead with it.

Helping the French was the fact that the black elites of French Africa had not achieved their elitism in spite of France, but in most cases, thanks to it. As a consequence, the relationship between France and her colonies was more fraternal, largely because there was a more promising crop of national leaders to choose from, and in general those leaders had a great deal to gain by retaining a strong, familial association with France. These were men who were already seated in the French national assembly, whose voices were acknowledged, who understood the intricacies of government, and who had been groomed over generations.

The Ivorian Houphouët-Boigny was the first among equals in this club. A landowner and a Christian parent, he was hardly the one to be waging war with France. Perhaps one of his most memorable comments in the matter of black self-determination in Africa was uttered at the 1958 opening of a trade fair in Côte d'Ivoire: "If you don't want to vegetate in bamboo huts, concentrate your efforts on growing good cocoa and coffee." In 1946, Houphouët-Boigny was 41. He had entered politics at a village and then municipal level, edging through the first cracks that were opening up in the tightly ethnocentric system being created by the birth of the French Union.

The Constitution of the Fourth Republic, representing perhaps the largest of those cracks and which had been adopted by referendum in October 1946, allowed for colonial representation in both houses of parliament. These amounted to seven percent of the seats of the National Assembly and 15% of those in the Council of the Republic. In addition, all the colonies were given limited indigenous authority through the formation of local assemblies that were empowered to debate and approve local budget items. In addition, a double-college system governing elections overseas was introduced, with one college for French expatriates and another for native people, albeit with the indigenous franchise limited to a tiny, educated elite. Furthermore, colonies were no longer referred to by that name, but as overseas territories, or territoires outremer.

Thus, black African deputies from each of these territories would sit as full and equal members of the French Assembly, defining their territories as integral to a united and indivisible republic. This was a bold framework that was at once pragmatic and optimistic. The British certainly did not venture to add provinces to the Kingdom, but sought instead to create a Commonwealth, loosening the empire by degrees and allying its past members through economic, military and cultural cooperation. Elected assemblies were established in each of the various French African territories, none with any particular authority, while the governors would remain disproportionally powerful. However, it was undeniable that local representation and administration in the colonies was substantially recognized in the new constitution, and a system of electoral politics established throughout.

This, many have argued, marked the precise moment that the 15-year journey towards full political independence in French Africa began. It was a far more benign journey than that fated for Portuguese colonies, and even more so for the Belgian Congo. In sub-Saharan Africa at least, the French imperial withdrawal triggered no significant civil wars and no notable wars of disengagement. Notwithstanding much pettifogging and cynicism in its application, and many trivial restrictions imposed at a local level to frustrate the spirit of the constitution, this act by France, extraordinarily generous for the times, had the effect of generating a broadly positive and pro-French sentiment throughout the African colonies. This view of things would aid France significantly in its efforts to remain active and relevant in Africa long after decolonization. Under a Francophone African union, France was (or ought to have been) in a stronger position even than Britain, which was already fighting the first of the wars of disengagement in Malaya, Cypress, and Kenya.

Another point worth remarking upon is that the establishment of broad-based electoral representation in the individual territories of French Africa was only really possible because of a long-standing tradition of political liberty. This ensured a corpus of experienced and educated black politicians, and a tradition of electoral politics for the French to hand over, and for indigenous leaderships to adopt. Other colonizing nations, Britain in particular, realizing by the 1950s that black rule in Africa was inevitable, tried to establish indigenous political institutions far too late to have any positive effect. Most transitions of power in British Africa were accompanied by some level of violence and civil unrest, which did not happen in the French territories of sub-Saharan Africa. For generations, France had nurtured the development of gifted Senegalese, so when the time came for the handover of power, men such as Léopold Sédar Senghor were standing ready to receive it.

A Free Senegal

"What if this were Hell, this absence of sleep, this poet's desert, this pain of living, this dying of not dying, this anguish of shadows, this passion over death and light." – Léopold Sédar Senghor

President de Gaulle was charged with the responsibility of making things work for the French, and while the British Empire was devolving into a Commonwealth, de Gaulle pictured a modern federal state that would include, as overseas members, France's African territories. In essence, de Gaulle put it to the crop of French African dependencies, now all looking on with anxious expectation to be told by *le Général* how the future would look, that two avenues of progress were open to them. The first was membership of the new French global union, or federation, along with which would come all the benefits of French political and economic patronage. The second was total independence from France, the rewards for which would be a severing of all links with France – social, political, and military, and most importantly for most, economic. "But what is inconceivable," de Gaulle said in a press interview on the matter, "is an independent state which France continues to help. If the choice is for independence, the government will draw, with regret, the conclusions that follow from the expression of that choice."

A constitutional referendum held in October 1958 revealed that of all France's African dependencies, only the territory of Guinea, led by the firebrand nationalist Ahmed Sékou Touré, was willing to venture into statehood unassisted. The French responded to this with stone-faced Gallic formality, removing all official personnel and everything of value to the new republic, serving notice on others observing that what de Gaulle said was what de Gaulle meant.

Meanwhile, Senghor was still in France when constitution of the Fourth Republic began to emerge from the ashes of Vichy France, and he was at last ready to lend his influence to the new face of France. By then he was a published poet, and his literary contributions were earning universally positive reviews. His name was known, and his voice was increasingly being heard. By then, naturally, he was extremely fluent in French academic life and society, and daily more influential in the Senegalese expatriate community. He was moderate, intellectual, and highly literate, so naturally he was chosen to be a consultative presence during the drafting of the constitution of the Fourth Republic. His first consultative appointment was to the *Monnerville*

Commission, chaired by the black Guianese lawyer Gaston Monnerville and mandated to look into and advise on the future status of all the French colonies.

Monnerville

It is worth noting here, however, that Senghor was the exception, not the rule. He was perhaps the best that the European colonial system had to offer, for although he had felt the usual pinpricks of racism, unlike many of the fiercely nationalistic, often Marxist and always intellectually aggressive liberation leaders springing up all over Africa, he had never been imprisoned, proscribed, or restricted, and probably only ever disrespected at the lowest levels of French society. He bore no animosity to France, had nothing to rebel against, and would have had everything to lose by estrangement.

Furthermore, while he may have been the highest profile Senegalese native in France at that time, Léopold Senghor was by no means the most senior. That position belonged to fifty-four-year old Lamine Guèye, a highly respected and extremely popular Senegalese lawyer resident north of Paris. Guèye was also founder and leader of the Senegalese Socialist Party, which was the dominant political force in Senegal, and Senghor himself was a senior member at that time.[5]

Naturally, it was widely assumed that Guèye would be appointed to stand as the main socialist candidate for the first of the two seats available to Senegal in the new French National Assembly. These were to represent both the *Communes* and the subject areas, and since Senghor had been born a subject, he was something of an obvious choice to be nominated as the socialist candidate for the second seat. The election of October 1945 produced the expected result, and the Guèye-Senghor partnership was duly consummated with a clean sweep.

---

[5] *Senegalese Socialist Party – Parti Socialiste Sénégalais –* was founded in July 1934.

Senghor claimed before and after this first post-war election that he was very reluctant to leave the comfort of academia to enter the rough-and-tumble of politics, which is perhaps understandable. He was on the cusp of an outstanding career, and also a little concerned as to how the fact that he was in a long-standing relationship with a white French woman might be received in Senegal. As it turned out, it did not appear to matter much. He and Guèye ran on a platform mostly free of revolutionary verbiage and strongly assimilationist in tone.

At the start of the 1950s, the situation in Kenya had degenerated into bloody rebellion, and everywhere an emerging black political movement was beginning to make its voice heard. By 1954, Indochina was shaking loose of French influence, and the Algerian War began shortly after that. The Belgians, fearing a similar war in the Congo, took the decision to hand over the colony as soon as possible, and to whomever was in place to receive it. In West Africa, the British were grooming their colonies for independence and struggling to control the enthusiasm, while the white regimes in Rhodesia and South Africa were beginning to build political and military ramparts against the inevitable.

Lamine Guèye was left with the diplomatic pleasures of Paris, while Senghor found himself worrying about the practical effects of all of this on French West Africa and Equatorial Africa, in particular in the event of an overly hasty French withdrawal. His principal concern was that the sudden collapse of the current West African and Equatorial Federations would have the effect of Balkanizing the region, which would in turn undermine the security and viability of everyone. At the root of it, he was not in favor of independence at all, but he was apt to present instead the idea of an expanded, federal amalgamation of Francophone African states, not as an independent entity, but forming part of a Greater France.

The French Union, however, survived only as long as the French Fourth Republic, from 1946-1958, and it achieved very little in terms of practical political development in Africa for a variety of reasons. The most important was perhaps the fact that the initial gratitude and magnanimity felt by metropolitan France towards the African colonies in the aftermath of World War II quickly began to fade, and with a hardening of attitudes in France came a deeper entrenchment of the colonial administrations and a general state of political deadlock within the colonies. Senghor now began to see the potential pitfalls of decolonization, and while he did not support it, he was prepared to acknowledge its inevitability. He tried to persuade his fellow West African leaders to form a region-wide political movement in recognition of the fact that territorial divisions would simply make it easier for the French to dominate and more difficult for Africans to federate and organize among themselves.

Senghor's fears of the Balkanization of West Africa were well founded, and this was simply because an emerging crop of black nationalists saw greater value in the presidency of a small nation than the governorship of a federated province. Senghor exhausted a great deal of energy and time trying to find a workable and politically viable strategy for achieving political cohesion in West Africa, but ultimately to little effect. At the time, he lacked the same prestige and same fire of politicians like Houphouët-Boigny, his chief rival as the guiding voice of Francophone African independence. Houphouët-Boigny was as ambitious as he was ruthless, and he had no interest in deferring his own premiership of an independent Côte d'Ivoire in the interests of a West African Federation. Also, as a student of realpolitik, he probably had a clearer sense of how improbable such a proposal ultimately was.

Throughout West Africa, the mood on the continent began to shift as the 1950s continued. Large numbers of young and educated blacks were emerging from the school systems and universities, merging with trained but underemployed men who had served in many capacities during World War II and returned to discover a home still dominated by the French. Ambitious leaders began to fret about the limitations of local government, and mass movements were easily stirred up upon the common grievance of occupation.

Senghor was fully aware of this movement, for he had, after all, been one of the principal architects of the black African awakening. Although he was subject to these potential currents of change and was forced to trim his sails often, and sail hard against a reactionary wind, he was never personally motivated by radical politics, for the simple reason that he bore no animus towards the French. His had not been an experience of oppression, and so his was not a policy of confrontation. Both he and Guèye had come as close to assimilation as was biologically possible at that time. Neither man was particularly fired by the verbiage of revolution, nor did they identify with the radicals and the Marxist-Leninist revolutionaries like Kwame Nkrumah, Patrice Lumumba, Agostinho Neto, and others beginning to rise and confront their colonial masters across Africa.

Despite these limitations, though, Senghor dominated the Senegalese political scene, and there was never any particular doubt he was the anointed leader of the local independence movement. Guèye was certainly not likely to abandon his town house in Saint-Denis in favor of the political trenches, so it was left entirely to Senghor to organize on behalf of the party back in Senegal.

Even as he was pleading his reluctance to enter the political fray, Senghor proved himself extremely capable, and he worked diligently and effectively to build a strong following in Senegal as independence approached. In 1948, he formed a breakaway political front, the *Bloc Démocratique Sénégalais* (BDS), choosing as his aide-de-camp a long-time friend and colleague, Mamadou Dia. He also organized, and quickly dominated the *Indépendants d'outré-mer* (IOM), a grouping of influential individuals among the growing caucus of African representatives in the French Chamber of Deputies.

The effectiveness of the *Bloc Démocratique Sénégalais* organization in Senegal offered ample proof that Senghor had acknowledged an independent Sengal was not far off in the future, and it now seemed he embraced the movement and was now driving forward with his own political ambitions. While the stated platform of the BDS remained commitment to the interests of

Senegal, and West Africa as a whole within the French Union, it also began to project an increasingly socialist and democratic message, with a strong flavor of nationalism and a clear independence agenda.

The first test of the BDS came with the 1951 French parliamentary elections, under the rules of which Senegal was qualified to elect two deputies. With a massive increase in educated youth now eligible, the emphasis of political activity in Senegal began to shift from the communes to the countryside, and it was here that Senghor came into his own. The BDS took both seats in the French Chamber, and 41 out of 50 seats in the local territorial assembly. Needless to say, Guèye lost his socialist seat to a *Bloc Démocratique Sénégalais* candidate, which represented a political earthquake to say the very least.

With this success behind him, Senghor began to respond to the mood of his constituency by injecting into his political rhetoric small but increasing doses of autonomy, and occasionally even independence. Of course, he remained careful to retain a moderate tone, and always he kept declaring unshakable loyalty to France. "To assimilate, but not to be assimilated" became his political mantra, implying quite obviously that while the black man might welcome the best of the French, it was not to be to the exclusion of himself. These would be the terms of Senegal's journey towards Senegalese independence, terms defined by the great poet and intellectual himself.

As he accrued influence in Senegal, Senghor was finally in a position to square up to the Goliath of the emerging block of indigenous West African power brokers: Félix Houphouët-Boigny. What emerged was a fitful political rivalry that would go back and forth for the next three decades.

Initially the disagreements between the two men took place against the broader backdrop of a continent-wide move towards independence. A temporary status was established with the implementation of the French Union, but beneath the surface the general debate continued to center on the long-term future of Africa. For the French, it was accepted that independence on some level would happen, but the insistence that it remain somehow within the French milieu made quite clear the French intended to remain influential in Africa. Thus, the extent of autonomy and the rate of devolution became the central themes of debate throughout the late 1950s.

The wave broke with the implementation in 1957 of the *Loi-cadre*, or the "Reform Act," a French legal reform that in essence transferred a critical load of authority from the central jurisdiction of Paris to the colonies themselves. This was a major step into what would succeed the French Union: the "French Community," comparable perhaps to the British Commonwealth. It would define the future relationship between France and her overseas territories upon the grant of independence. The devolution of power, incidentally, was not to the capital of the existing French West African Federation, Dakar, as Senghor would have preferred, but to the capitals of each individual colony. There would be no grand Francophone African federation.

Much of the impetus for the introduction of the *Loi-cadre*, and the apparent willingness of the French to cede to black demands of independence in Africa, lay in the French defeat in Indochina and the outbreak of violence in Algeria. These were events that deeply unsettled the leadership of the Fourth Republic which then went to great lengths to avoid any similar events in sub-Saharan Africa. While the drafting of the *Loi-cadre* might have been a landmark on the journey of Francophone Africa towards independence, more than anything it was a landmark victory for Houphouët-Boigny.

Senghor and Houphouët-Boigny wrestled over one key point: the issue of an inter-territorial party to represent French West African interests as a whole. This would aim to create a tighter regional union, perhaps even a federation of French West African states, to avoid the Balkanization of West Africa that Senghor feared most. The battle was waged in the various African sub-committees of the Chamber of Deputies, where, unfortunately for Senghor's vision of a federated West Africa, Houphouët-Boigny was the stronger presence. Houphouët-Boigny led the *Rassemblement Démocratique Africain* (RDA), and Senghor continued leading the IOM.

The showdown took place with the French parliamentary election of 1956, from which Houphouët-Boigny and his RDA block emerged the clear winner. For Senghor and his IOM, it was an abject defeat. Only six allied sitting deputies were returned. For Houphouët-Boigny the laurels of victory included a cabinet position in France as a minister without portfolio and a seat on the drafting committee of the *Loi-cadre*, giving him the latitude to influence the design of a future West Africa and practically exclude Senghor from that process.

Then, on May 13, 1958, the French army in Algeria staged a revolt, and for a while France itself hovered on the brink of a coup. The Fourth Republic collapsed, General Charles de Gaulle was recalled to power, and once again it was time to devise a new constitution.

As a cabinet minister, Houphouët-Boigny was present during all the working sessions to draft the constitution of the Fifth Republic, while Senghor, who had refused a cabinet position in the Debré Government, was able to contribute only as one of three African members of the constitutional consultative committee.[6] The result was that Houphouët-Boigny once again outmaneuvered the federalists, Senghor key among them, pressing his preferred confederal structure with no intermediate authority between the individual territories and France.

The net result was an acceleration of the devolution of powers to the individual colonies which further undermined the two federations of French West and French Equatorial Africa. The logic of this policy was simply that, with the removal of direct French control, the federations would be weak and unsustainable, and would very likely collapse into mutually antagonistic entities.

---

[6] Michel Jean-Pierre Debré was the first Prime Minister of the French Fifth Republic.

No doubt part of the French reasoning in backing the policy was that smaller, disunited territories would be easier for France to manage and control indirectly through the distribution of aid and military support.

Thus was born the short lived "French Community," based on almost absolute autonomy of the individual members, with metropolitan influence exerted through a common President, the President of France, who would retain substantial powers over such matters as unified defense, external affairs, currency, economic policy and strategic minerals, and a handful of other lesser but generally strategic concerns. The entire blueprint was only really superficially different from that of the *Loi-cadre*.

The ratification of the new constitution would be through a referendum held in each territory. De Gaulle adopted an uncompromising attitude on the matter of acceptance. It would be either "yes" or "no." It was made clear to the individual states that a "yes" vote would be a vote for the continuity of a supportive relationship with France, and a "no" vote would be an invitation for a complete severance of all governmental, civic, and military relations with France. Such a state would effectively be disinherited by France and would thereafter be completely on its own. When asked by Senghor what the consequences of a "no" vote would be, de Gaulle is said to have replied that "that territory will have seceded and would be from then on be considered foreign. France will know how to draw all the consequences from that choice."

On the day of the referendum, September 28, 1958, Senghor led Senegal to an overwhelmingly "yes" vote. There was a great deal of disquiet in the community at the stark terms of the referendum, and varying degrees of anger and disappointment about the French attitude, but only French Guinea and its firebrand leader Ahmed Sékou Touré voted "no." The consequences for Guinea were immediate, but Touré had employed a prophetic slogan: "We prefer poverty in liberty to riches in slavery" Guinea was immediately made an example of through an absolute and total removal of French money, materiel, investment, and aid. Guinea was abruptly left high and dry, and notwithstanding a quiet plea by Touré for forgiveness and inclusion, Guinea was removed from the family of French nations in Africa.

For his part, Senghor remained deeply disappointed in the lack of provision in the constitution for any kind of federal amalgamation in West Africa. He did not, however, abandon his quest, and he was successful to a degree in uniting the territory of Senegal with modern day Mali, then known as French Sudan, into a federation briefly called the Mali Federation. Other Francophone territories refused to join, however, largely in respect of Houphouët-Boigny's opposition to it. Ultimately, the Mali Federation limped along for the two-year life of the French Community before it essentially died from disunity soon afterwards.

Senghor quietly led Senegal out of the union in acceptance of the fact that federation in West Africa as a concept was doomed. The Mali Federation did, however, help catalyze the final phase of French disengagement from Africa, thanks to the federation's demand in September 1959 for independence from France. This was granted with limited conditions, left typically vague by de Gaulle, but which in principle prompted a rush of similar claims across the region.

In 1960, general independence was granted across French Africa under almost no political terms, and under formulas individually designed to achieve the optimum balance of full political autonomy with ongoing French interest. On September 6, 1960, Senghor was elected to the highest office in Senegal as its first independent president.

Senghor's ascension to the highest office in an independent Senegal was not only a personal triumph, but also a triumph of French policy for the century or more that had preceded this moment. It is natural that the institution of colonialism in Africa in general should be condemned, and there has been much to question and criticize about French colonization in general, but the fact is that Senegal as a territory, for reasons already described, attracted special conditions.

The status of the *Communes*, although not perfectly non-racial by any means, offered unique opportunities for men like Senghor, Diagne, and Guèye to educate themselves and to merge as much as was possible with the highest political and academic strata of the Métropole. This not only allowed these men and others like them to reach their full potential, but it offered the opportunity that was wholly lacking in many other regions of Africa for a class of black political elite to develop early in order to be poised to assume power when that moment came. It meant a more educated and erudite political class, deeply rooted political institutions, and a sense of personal investment in the stability and rationale of African independence.

This contrasts steeply with British, Portuguese and Belgian colonial practice, which tended to restrict black development and was generally hostile from the 1940s-1960s. The results of that behavior were that the black moderates were marginalized, sidelined, imprisoned, exiled, or assassinated, leaving political space open only to the radicals and offering only the lowest standards of racial integration when the time came to hand over power. Instability spread due to inexperience, as did misrule, corruption, violence, and one-party dictatorships. In several cases, military coups quickly followed hastily formed black governments, leading to the emergence of kleptocratic leadership cliques that were often supported by one superpower or another depending on the dicator's political leanings. These leaders damaged the economic viability of their nations, and the human rights records were appalling.

Notwithstanding some exceptions, such as the Central African Republic under Jean Bedel Bokassa, such adverse experiences did not occur in Francophone Africa. Indeed, the comparative moderation of Senghor's 20 years in office was a model of successful post-independence governance in Africa. His political style tended to follow closely his academic and literary development, leaning on the philosophical principles of negritude, black cultural autonomy, and an almost obsessive determination to retain the friendship and support of France. There was no radicalism in Senghor, and not a single note of nationalistic anger aimed at the French was ever heard in his rhetoric. He concerned himself with the lofty principles of democracy and the finer points of the Franco-Senegalese relationship, while the application of policy and practice was left to his deputy, Prime Minister Mamadou Dia, who was highly technocratic, somewhat doctrinaire, and personally ascetic. There was a strong socialistic flavor to Dia's policies that favored collectivism in agriculture, among other policies, which, although highly popular and successful at the grassroots level, tended to alienate the central business elite. That also comprised the political elite, and it certainly did not favor the entrenched French business interests that Senghor went out of his way to cultivate.

Dia

Senghor himself lapsed somewhat into the behavior that he had so criticized in Diagne and Guèye by indulging himself in the abstract pleasures of high political office while ignoring, or at least avoiding, the blunt practicalities of rule. This ought not to imply that he was detached, however. The displeasure felt in the local parliament at Dia's experimentation reached a head in 1962, when a political crisis erupted upon the introduction of a motion of censure against Dia for retaining a state of emergency in the country. It was believed the state of emergency was in place to allow Dia to rule more or less by decree. Dia at this time, among other portfolios, held the office of Minister of Defense, and it resulted in political jostling with Senghor that appeared likely for a time to end with a military coup. Things came to a head with Dia's arrest, trial, and eventual imprisonment for life (although in the end he served only 12 years under relatively liberal conditions).

This proved, if such proof was needed, that when push came to shove, Senghor did possess the type of Machiavellian instincts to outmaneuver and ultimately remove from the picture an ex-ally who had become obstructive to his rule. A certain capacity to maneuver was a basic prerequisite to survival in late 20th century Africa, and Senghor certainly did survive. His rule, however, continued to be abstruse, academic in tone, and perhaps a little too esoteric for the consumption of the masses. His continued involvement with the French, the constant influence of the French in Senegal, and his growing detachment to politics all tended to suggest that he was losing touch.

In recognition of this, Senghor adjusted the constitution to allow him to retire in favor of a deputy, at which point he began to groom his successor. This he found in young Abdou Diouf, who was similar in many respects to Mamadou Dia. A technocrat and loyal functionary, Prime Minister Diouf held that role until January 1, 1981, when Senghor resigned in favor of Diouf. Two years later, Diouf won a presidential election, assuming power in his own right.

Diouf

This marked yet another significant moment for Africa, as Senghor was the first substantive African leader to relinquish power voluntarily. Although his legitimacy had been eroded and the time to abdicate was right, there were many others of his generation who likewise reached that point and attempted through the imposition of one party states or other devices of dictatorship to remain in power. Diouf would repeat what Senghor did about 20 years later, reinforcing the point that the institutions of democracy in Senegal had been well founded, were deeply rooted, and would not be overturned easily.

In retirement, Senghor was at last able to return to the arts and academia, and his own living embodiment of negritude as a working, breathing philosophy. The crowning achievement of his life was his induction as a member of *l'Académie française* on June 2, 1983, where he succeeded Antoine de Lévis Mirepoix, a French historian, novelist, and essayist. Senghor was the first African to sit at the *Académie*. The last years of his life were spent with his wife in Verson, near the city of Caen in Normandy, where he died on December 20, 2001. His funeral was held on December 29, 2001 in Dakar.

Françafrique

"To speak a language is to take on a world, a culture." – Frantz Fanon

Despite being occupied by Nazi Germany during World War II, France was given a permanent seat on the United Nations Security Council, and despite the provisions set forth by President Roosevelt in the Atlantic Charter, which essentially made British Prime Minister Winston Churchill promise to dismantle the British Empire after the war, the United States supported the retention of France's overseas empire simply to avoid the possibility of having it fall quickly under the influence of the Soviet Union. In a sense, the French would be attempting to maintain influence in Africa to make sure political adversaries couldn't take advantage of any power vacuum either.

De Gaulle took enormous care to design a post-independence relationship with the departing African colonies to ensure continued French involvement in Africa, and to ensure that the former colonies supported France's interests and actions on the Security Council. Ultimately, Houphouët-Boigny coined the term *France-Afrique* to describe the unique relationship between Côte d'Ivoire and France, and it was later trimmed down to *Françafrique*.

The essential pillars of *Françafrique* were economic and military, and the job of assembling the intricate building blocks of this relationship was entrusted to Jacques Foccart, Chief of Staff for African affairs under both de Gaulle and Georges Pompidou. *La Foque*, as he was better known, was in charge of African affairs from 1960-1974, and it was he who negotiated all of the most important French-African political accords and treaties. He also directed the African activities of the Service de Documentation *Extérieure et de Contre-Espionnage*, the French external intelligence agency. He was very close to most African leaders, and as such, the whole business relied on cronyism and always remained opaque.

Foccart

The dealings may have been shady, but they resulted in a currency union that saw the *franc de la Communauté Financière Africaine*, or the CFA, pegged to the French Franc, with its convertibility guaranteed by the French central bank. There were numerous other features of this arrangement, but in practical terms it created a mutuality that, while tending to favor the French, offered a fair amount of economic stability on a sizable stretch of a continent that did not have a reputation for stability in the late 20th century.

The various cooperation accords were underpinned by a common defense agreement which granted the French enormous influence and freedom of action in terms of military presence and response to any common threat or individual crisis. Indeed, French military intervention Africa has been a far greater feature of French foreign policy than it has been for other previous imperial powers. Some 122 French military operation are listed in the period from 1960, with more than one major intervention every year between 1960 and the mid-1990s. Military cooperation also involved training and arms supply, as well as numerous threads of intelligence sharing and logistical collaboration.

The most important era for *Françafrique* was the Cold War, which served to limit the political influence of the Soviet Union and China in Francophone Africa. The communist powers had significant influence in the liberation wars raging across Africa, as well as many of the subsequent civil wars, coups, and military dictatorships that immediately followed the liberation era. Conversely, at the first sign of trouble, French troops were usually the first to arrive to prevent any unrest from turning into a major crisis. French garrisons were (and still are) located in Djibouti, Senegal, and Gabon, poised to respond quickly to any crisis. In some instances, these interventions protected regimes, such as in 1964, when French forces prevented a coup in Gabon. However, they have also toppled and replaced regimes periodically, as in Chad and the Central African Republic. Lately, French forces have been used to bolster the locals' capability to deal with jihadists in the Sahel region.

In the aftermath of the Cold War, the cohesion of *Françafrique* began to wear somewhat at the edges. This makes sense, given that the maturity of African states and their governments over time would need to rely less on the French, Moreover, they've had the freedom to establish local economic and military alliances, which also changed the political dynamics.

Nonetheless, the relationship between France and its former African colonies remains uniquely functional, and while the history of French colonialism is justifiably subjected to all kinds of criticism, *Françafrique* is still in existence.

Online Resources

Other books about African history by Charles River Editors

Other books about Senegal on Amazon

Further Reading

Aldrich, Robert. Greater France: A History of French Overseas Expansion (1996)

Atkinson, David. "Constructing Italian Africa: Geography and Geopolitics." Italian colonialism (2005): 15–26.

Axelson, Eric. Portugal and the Scramble for Africa: 1875–1891 (Johannesburg, Witwatersrand UP, 1967)

Boddy-Evans, Alistair. "What Caused the Scramble for Africa?" African History (2012). online

Brantlinger, Patrick. "Victorians and Africans: The genealogy of the myth of the dark continent." Critical Inquiry (1985): 166–203. online

Chamberlain, Muriel Evelyn. The scramble for Africa (4th ed. Routledge, 2014) excerpt and text search

Curtin, Philip D. Disease and empire: The health of European Troops in the Conquest of Africa (Cambridge University Press, 1998)

Darwin, John. "Imperialism and the Victorians: The dynamics of territorial expansion." English Historical Review (1997) 112#447 pp: 614–642.

Finaldi, Giuseppe. Italian National Identity in the Scramble for Africa: Italy's African Wars in the Era of Nation-building, 1870–1900 (Peter Lang, 2009)

Gjersø, Jonas Fossli (2015). "The Scramble for East Africa: British Motives Reconsidered, 1884-95." Journal of Imperial and Commonwealth History. Taylor & Francis. 43 (5): 831–60. doi:10.1080/03086534.2015.1026131. Retrieved 4 March 2016.

Hammond, Richard James. Portugal and Africa, 1815–1910: a study in uneconomic imperialism (Stanford University Press, 1966)

Henderson, W. O. The German Colonial Empire, 1884–1919 (London: Frank Cass, 1993)

Hochschild, Adam (2006) [1998]. King Leopold's Ghost: A Story of Greed, Terror, and Heroism in Colonial Africa. London: Pan Books. ISBN 978-0-330-44198-8.

Klein, Martin A. Slavery and colonial rule in French West Africa (Cambridge University Press, 1998)

Lovejoy, Paul E. Transformations in slavery: a history of slavery in Africa (Cambridge University Press, 2011)

Lloyd, Trevor Owen. Empire: the history of the British Empire (2001).

Mackenzie J. M. The Partition of Africa, 1880–1900, and European Imperialism in the Nineteenth Century (London 1983).

Oliver, Roland, Sir Harry Johnston and the Scramble for Africa (1959) online

Pakenham, Thomas (1992) [1991]. The Scramble for Africa. London: Abacus. ISBN 978-0-349-10449-2.

Penrose E. F., ed. European Imperialism and the Partition of Africa (London 1975).

Perraudin, Michael, and Jürgen Zimmerer, eds. German colonialism and national identity (London: Taylor & Francis, 2010)

Robinson R,. and J. Gallagher, "The partition of Africa", in The New Cambridge Modern History vol XI, pp 593–640 (Cambridge, 1962).

Rotberg, Robert I. The Founder: Cecil Rhodes and the Pursuit of Power (1988) excerpt and text search; online

Sanderson G. N., "The European partition of Africa: Coincidence or conjuncture?" Journal of Imperial and Commonwealth History (1974) 3#1 pp 1–54.

Sparrow-Niang, J., Bath and the Nile Explorers: In commemoration of the 150th anniversary of Burton and Speke's encounter in Bath, September 1864, and their 'Nile Duel' which never happened(Bath: Bath Royal Literary & Scientific Institution, 2014)

Stoecker, Helmut. German imperialism in Africa: From the beginnings until the Second World War (Hurst & Co., 1986.)

Thomas, Antony. Rhodes: The Race for Africa (1997) excerpt and text search

Thompson, Virginia, and Richard Adloff. French West Africa (Stanford University Press, 1958)

Wesseling, H.L. and Arnold J. Pomerans. Divide and rule: The partition of Africa, 1880–1914 (Praeger, 1996.)

Free Books by Charles River Editors

We have brand new titles available for free most days of the week. To see which of our titles are currently free, click on this link.

Discounted Books by Charles River Editors

We have titles at a discount price of just 99 cents everyday. To see which of our titles are currently 99 cents, click on this link.